COMPOSER'S Choice

RANDALL HARTSELL

T0079508

ABOUT THE SERIES

The Composer's Choice series showcases piano works by an exclusive group of composers. Each collection contains classic piano pieces that were carefully chosen by the composer, as well as brand-new pieces written especially for the series. Helpful performance notes are also included.

ISBN 978-1-4803-5457-9

WILLIS MUSIC

Exclusively Distributed By

HAL•LEONARD®
CORPORATION
7777 W. BLUEMOUND RD. P.O. BOX 13819 MILWAUKEE, WI 53213

Visit Hal Leonard Online at
www.halleonard.com

FROM THE COMPOSER

I have enjoyed selecting both old favorites and new compositions for this collection. The earlier pieces are like old friends that I am happy to see again. I am pleased to introduce new lyrical music to your studio as well. I hope some of these pieces will become standards in your music library for a long time to come. Enjoy!

Randall Hartsell

CONTENTS

RIVER DANCE

This dynamic and energetic composition uses movable five-finger positions, accents and *staccatos*. Students should practice playing harmonic 5ths with each hand in the key positions of C, B♭ and A♭. Practice clapping the rhythms in measures 1-2 and 17-18, and perhaps try playing all the rhythms on a drum or rhythm instrument. Be sure to contrast the smooth *legato* versus crisp *staccato* passages in measures 17-24.

From what country do you imagine this composition originated?

TIDES OF TAHITI

The melodic line is indicated by tenuto marks. Bring out the moving notes of each chord and use clear, syncopated pedal changes. Imagine beautiful turquoise waters and warm, gentle breezes to make this music come alive.

SUNSET IN MADRID

An understanding of expressive, lyrical *legato* playing and balance between the hands is required. Visualize the melody being played by a violin, a flute, or even sung. While playing the left hand chords quietly, listen for all the notes to sound in each chord. Also, try playing just the left hand and singing the melody. As you perform, envision yourself in sunny Madrid!

RAIDERS IN THE NIGHT

Contrasts in mood, dynamics and touch make this piece dramatic and fun to perform.

Section A utilizes octaves and accents. Be sure that the arms move smoothly over the keyboard and with ease. Use arm weight to play clear, bright accents. Listen for contrasts between the *legato* right hand and *staccato* left-hand passages.

Section B is more lyrical in nature. First, practice the left hand in blocked chords. Next, practice the right hand and listen for a beautiful melodic line. Put both hands together and only add pedal after you can play the piece securely and up to tempo. Play with energy and conviction.

SHOWERS AT DAYBREAK

Revisiting this composition is like sharing coffee with an old friend. Play it in a reflective manner and experiment with bringing out the subtle nuances of each phrase.

Listen for clear pedal changes and place enough weight on the melodic line to allow it to sing above the other voices. Your ear should lead you to bring out other voices as well. Good phrasing is so important when playing four-part harmony.

ABOVE THE CLOUDS

D Major is my favorite key. I love its bright, cheerful sound, especially when played in the very middle of the piano keyboard. Play the melodic line and do a little analysis. Where does the introduction end and section A begin? Be sure the notes that are played with the thumb blend in with the other notes and are not too heavy. The tenuto notes in section B indicate the melodic line, so listen for a rich tone in these notes. As usual, clear pedal changes are important, and good control of balance is essential. Soar above the clouds in the warm sunlight of a beautiful and satisfying performance.

SUNBURSTS IN THE RAIN

I love choosing creative titles, expressive melodic lines, and harmonic and melodic sequences. This composition captures many of my favorite things. Practice the left hand with pedal. Notice the patterns and listen to the harmonic conversation. The right-hand phrases should sound "conversational." Section B begins softly with the tied melodic notes and will require a rich tone to sustain the ties. Notice the hemiola created in the last line of this composition: it blurs the rhythmic pulse and creates a pleasant ending to this gentle shower.

AUTUMN REVERIE

"Autumn Reverie" uses three motives that reflect the gorgeous colors and subtle hues in the fall season—see if you can find them. Reveal the beauty of the season through clear pedal changes and sensitive *cantabile* playing.

River Dance

Randall Hartsell

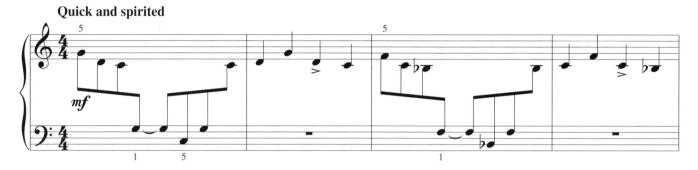

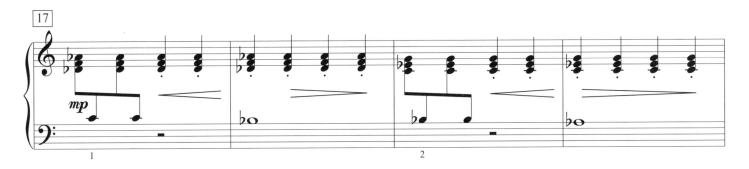

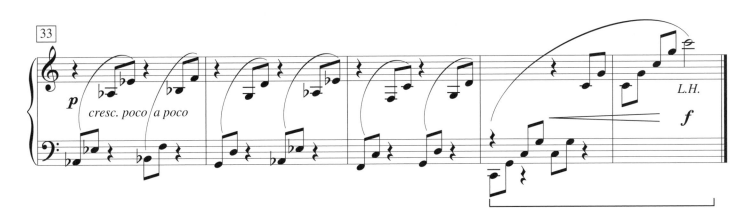

Tides of Tahiti

Randall Hartsell

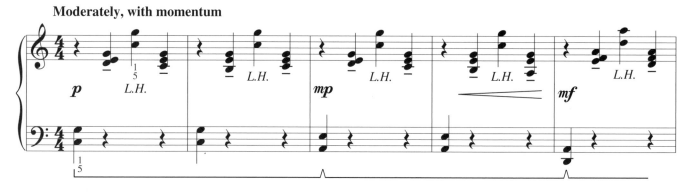

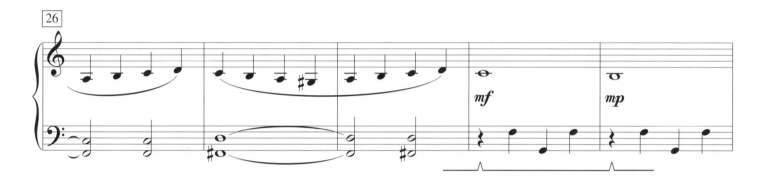

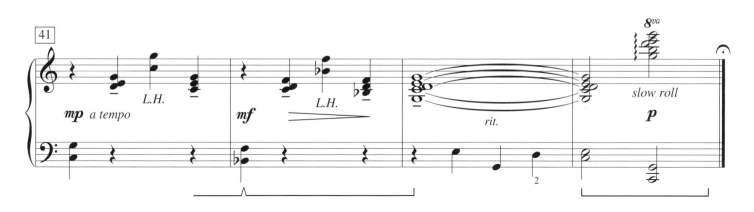

Sunset in Madrid

Randall Hartsell

Moderately and expressively

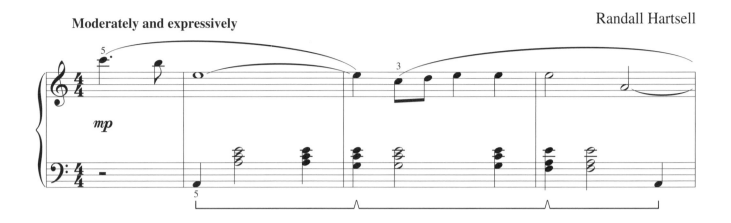

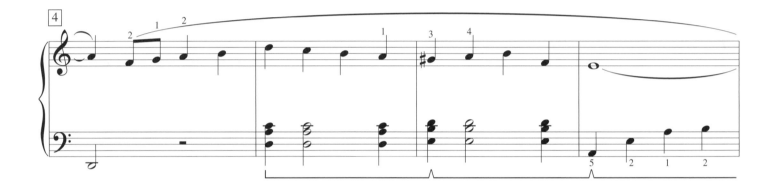

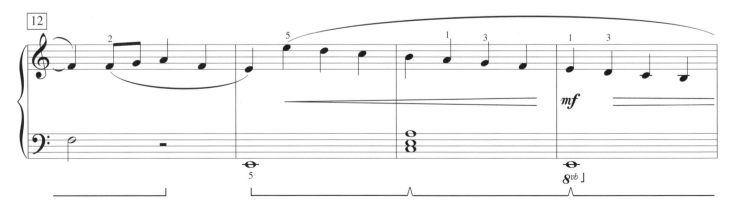

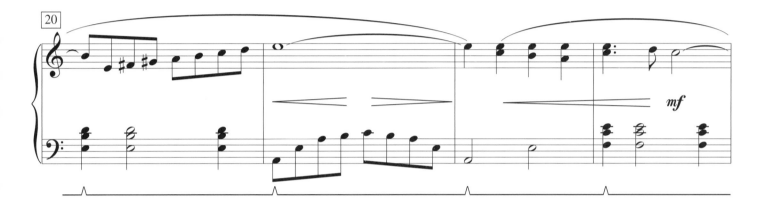

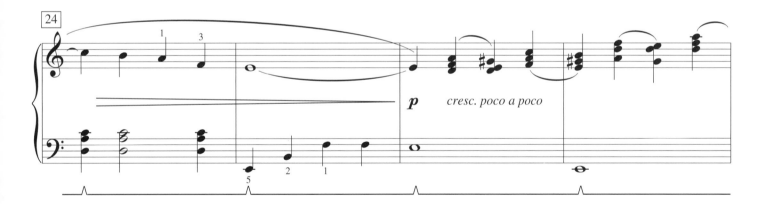

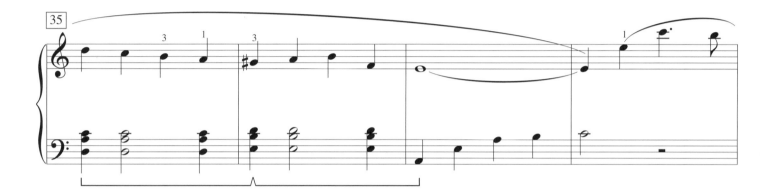

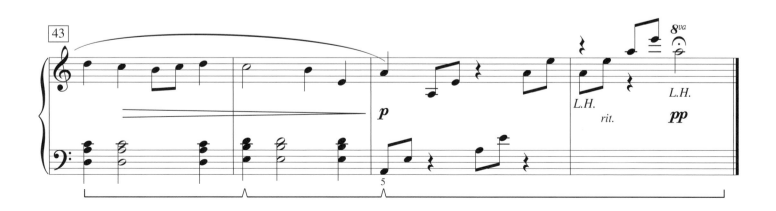

Raiders in the Night

Randall Hartsell

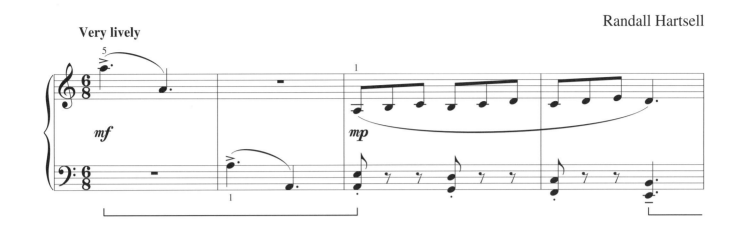

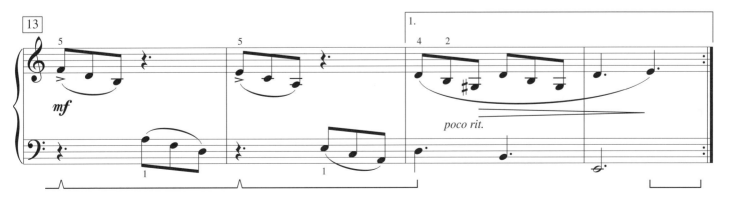

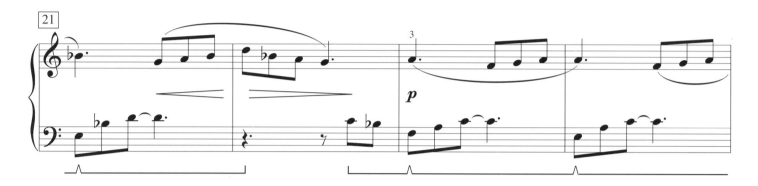

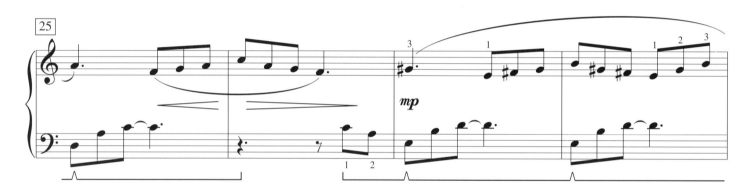

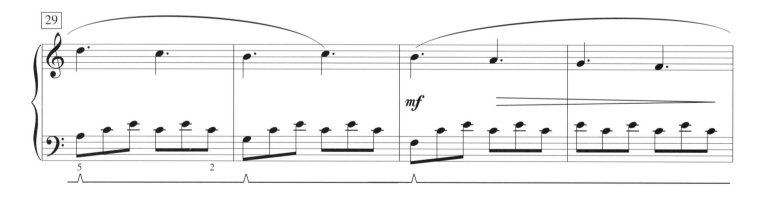

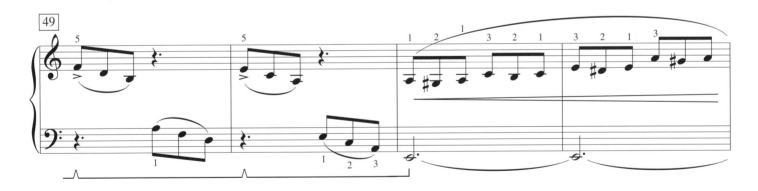

Showers at Daybreak

Randall Hartsell

Moderately and freely

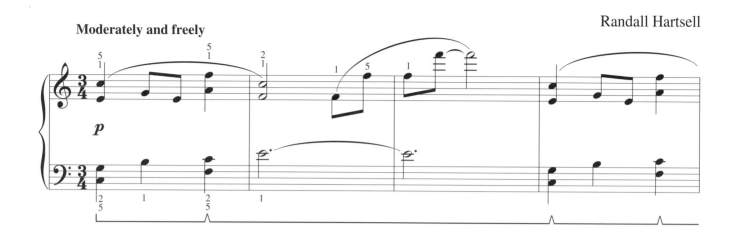

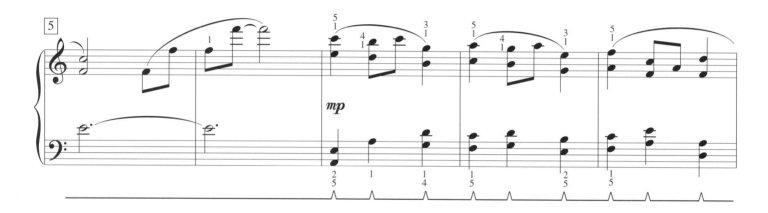

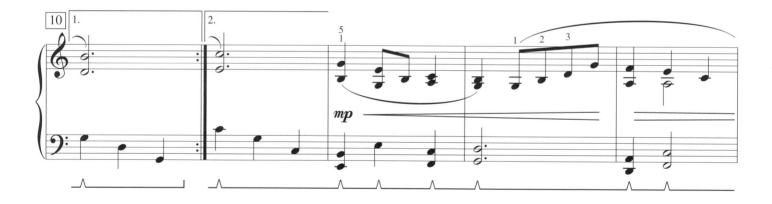

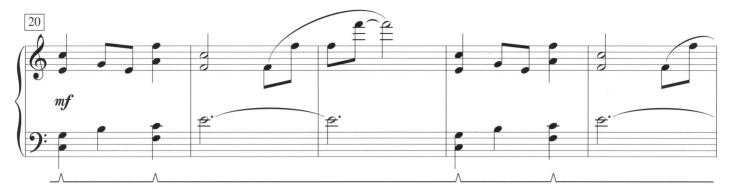

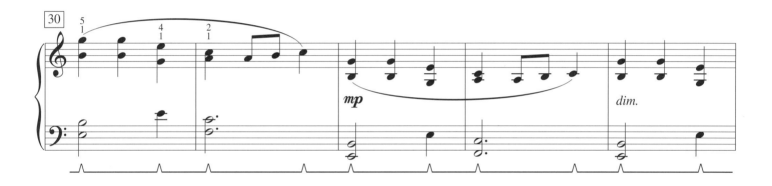

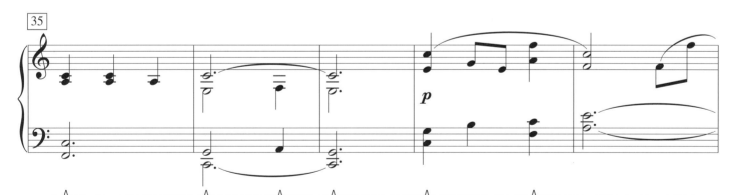

Above the Clouds

Randall Hartsell

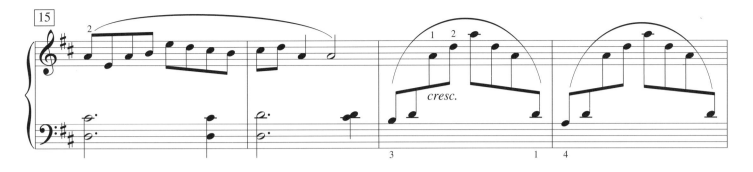

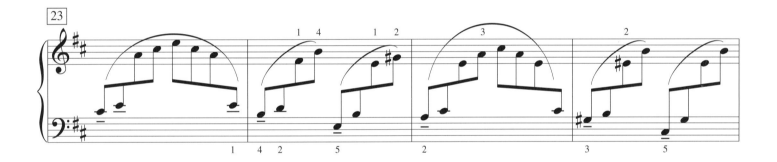

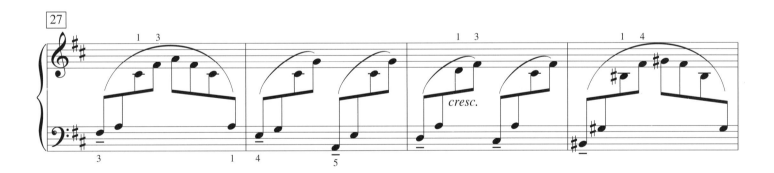

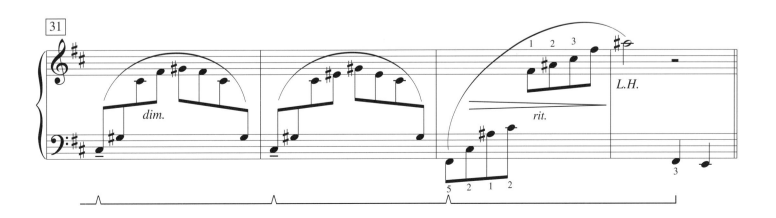

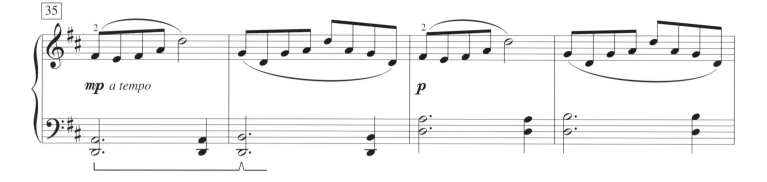

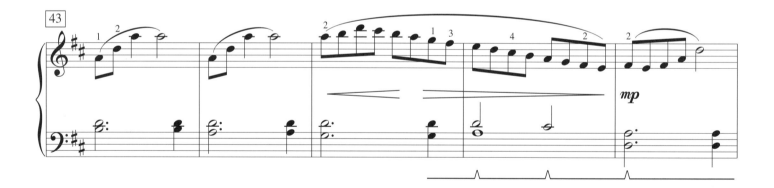

To my inspiring teacher, Robert Carter

Sunbursts in the Rain

Randall Hartsell

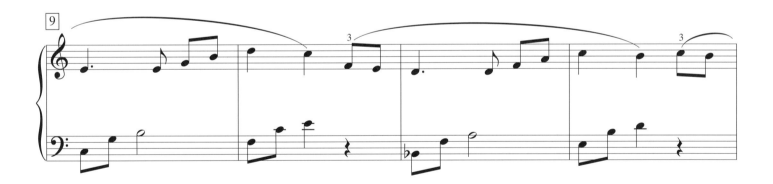

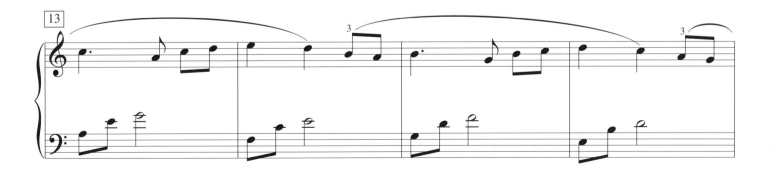

22

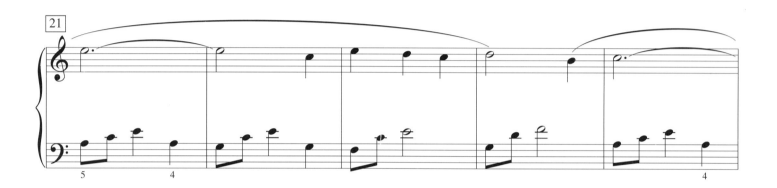

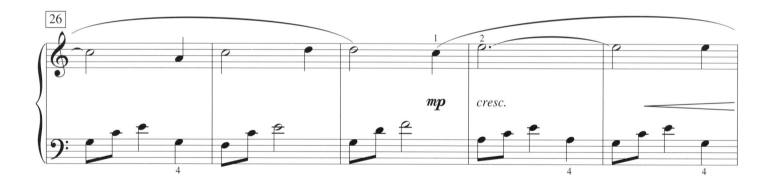

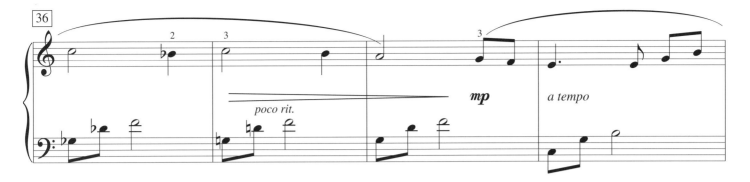

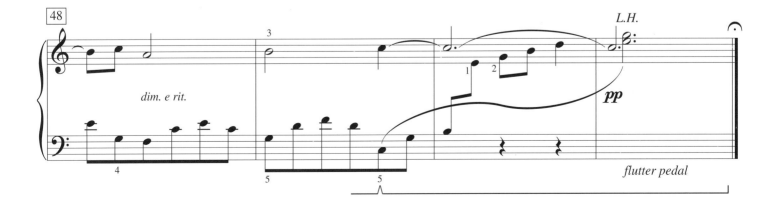

Autumn Reverie

Randall Hartsell

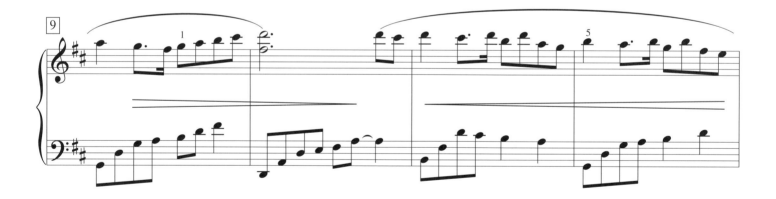

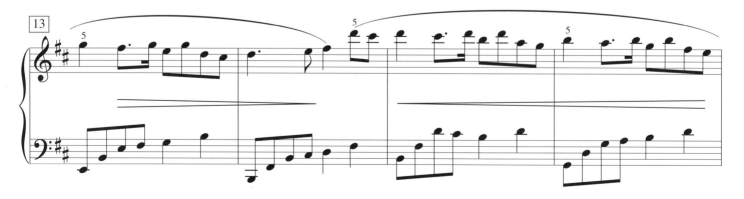

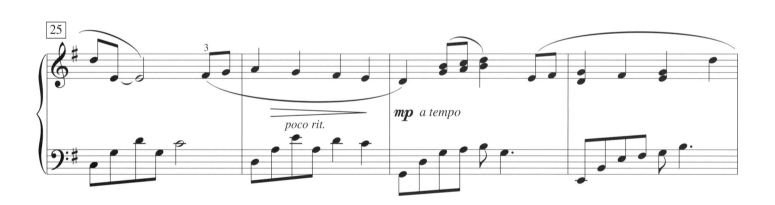

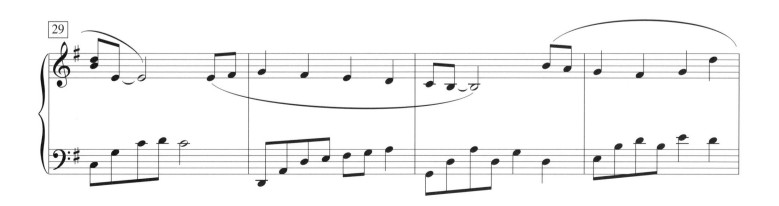

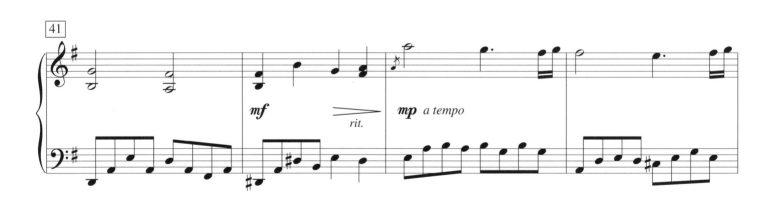

CLASSIC PIANO REPERTOIRE

The *Classic Piano Repertoire* series includes popular as well as lesser-known pieces from a select group of composers out of the Willis piano archives. Every piece has been newly engraved and edited with the aim to preserve each composer's original intent and musical purpose.

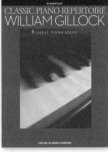

WILLIAM GILLOCK – ELEMENTARY

8 Great Piano Solos

Dance in Ancient Style • Little Flower Girl of Paris • On a Paris Boulevard • Rocking Chair Blues • Sliding in the Snow • Spooky Footsteps • A Stately Sarabande • Stormy Weather.

00416957 .... $8.99

EDNA MAE BURNAM – ELEMENTARY

8 Great Piano Solos

The Clock That Stopped • The Friendly Spider • A Haunted House • New Shoes • The Ride of Paul Revere • The Singing Cello • The Singing Mermaid • Two Birds in a Tree.

00110228 .... $8.99

JOHN THOMPSON – ELEMENTARY

9 Great Piano Solos

Captain Kidd • Drowsy Moon • Dutch Dance • Forest Dawn • Humoresque • Southern Shuffle • Tiptoe • Toy Ships • Up in the Air.

00111968 .... $8.99

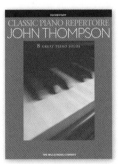

LYNN FREEMAN OLSON – EARLY TO LATER ELEMENTARY

14 Great Piano Solos

Caravan • Carillon • Come Out! Come Out! (Wherever You Are) • Halloween Dance • Johnny, Get Your Hair Cut! • Jumping the Hurdles • Monkey on a Stick • Peter the Pumpkin Eater • Pony Running Free • Silent Shadows • The Sunshine Song • Tall Pagoda • Tubas and Trumpets • Winter's Chocolatier.

00294722 .... $9.99

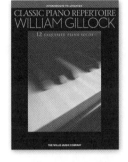

WILLIAM GILLOCK – INTERMEDIATE TO ADVANCED

12 Exquisite Piano Solos

Classic Carnival • Etude in A Major (The Coral Sea) • Etude in E Minor • Etude in G Major (Toboggan Ride) • Festive Piece • A Memory of Vienna • Nocturne • Polynesian Nocturne • Sonatina in Classic Style • Sonatine • Sunset • Valse Etude.

00416912 .... $12.99

EDNA MAE BURNAM – INTERMEDIATE TO ADVANCED

13 Memorable Piano Solos

Butterfly Time • Echoes of Gypsies • Hawaiian Leis • Jubilee! • Longing for Scotland • Lovely Senorita • The Mighty Amazon River • Rumbling Rumba • The Singing Fountain • Song of the Prairie • Storm in the Night • Tempo Tarantelle • The White Cliffs of Dover.

00110229 .... $12.99

JOHN THOMPSON – INTERMEDIATE TO ADVANCED

12 Masterful Piano Solos

Andantino (from Concerto in D Minor) • The Coquette • The Faun • The Juggler • Lagoon • Lofty Peaks • Nocturne • Rhapsody Hongroise • Scherzando in G Major • Tango Carioca • Valse Burlesque • Valse Chromatique.

00111969 .... $12.99

LYNN FREEMAN OLSON – EARLY TO MID-INTERMEDIATE

13 Distinctive Piano Solos

Band Wagon • Brazilian Holiday • Cloud Paintings • Fanfare • The Flying Ship • Heroic Event • In 1492 • Italian Street Singer • Mexican Serenade • Pageant Dance • Rather Blue • Theme and Variations • Whirlwind.

00294720 .... $9.99

WILLIS MUSIC

EXCLUSIVELY DISTRIBUTED BY

HAL•LEONARD®

CLOSER LOOK View sample pages and hear audio excerpts online at **www.halleonard.com**

www.willispianomusic.com

 www.facebook.com/willispianomusic

Prices, content, and availability subject to change without notice.

A DOZEN A DAY SONGBOOK SERIES

BROADWAY, MOVIE AND POP HITS

Arranged by Carolyn Miller

The *A Dozen a Day Songbook* series contains wonderful Broadway, movie and pop hits that may be used as companion pieces to the memorable technique exercises in the *A Dozen a Day* series. They are also suitable as supplements for ANY method!

MINI
EARLY ELEMENTARY
Songs in the Mini Book:
Any Dream Will Do • Can You Feel the Love Tonight • A Dream Is a Wish Your Heart Makes • Heigh-Ho • I'm Popeye the Sailor Man • It's a Grand Night for Singing • Lean on Me • Love Me Tender • So Long, Farewell • You'll Never Walk Alone.

00416858 Book Only $9.99

00416861 Book/Audio $12.99

PREPARATORY
MID-ELEMENTARY
Songs in the Preparatory Book:
The Bare Necessities • Do-Re-Mi • Getting to Know You • Heart and Soul • Little April Shower • Part of Your World • The Surrey with the Fringe on Top • Swinging on a Star • The Way You Look Tonight • Yellow Submarine.

00416859 Book Only $9.99

00416862 Book/Audio $12.99

BOOK 1
LATER ELEMENTARY
Songs in Book 1:
Cabaret • Climb Ev'ry Mountain • Give a Little Whistle • If I Were a Rich Man • Let It Be • Rock Around the Clock • Twist and Shout • The Wonderful Thing About Tiggers • Yo Ho (A Pirate's Life for Me) • Zip-A-Dee-Doo-Dah.

00416860 Book Only $9.99

00416863 Book/Audio $12.99

BOOK 2
EARLY INTERMEDIATE
Songs in Book 2:
Hallelujah • I Dreamed A Dream • I Walk the Line • I Want to Hold Your Hand • In the Mood • Moon River • Once Upon A Dream • This Land is Your Land • A Whole New World • You Raise Me Up.

00119241 Book Only $9.99

00119242 Book/Audio $14.99

Prices, content, and availability subject to change without notice.

EXCLUSIVELY DISTRIBUTED BY

HAL•LEONARD®

Spectacular Piano Solos

from

www.willispianomusic.com

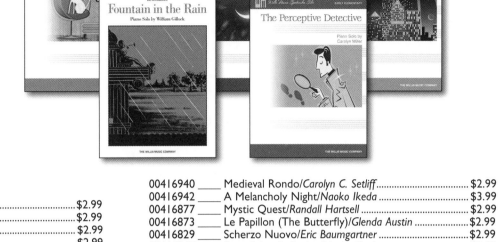

7777 W. BLUEMOUND RD. P.O. BOX 13819 MILWAUKEE, WI 53213

CLOSER LOOK View sample pages and hear audio excerpts online at **www.halleonard.com**

www.facebook.com/willispianomusic

Prices & availability subject to change without notice.